Now Is Where We Are

Poems from the Priory Hospital

by

Hilary Lissenden

Augur Press

British Library Cataloguing in Publication Data.
A catalogue record for this book is available from the
British Library.

ISBN 978-0-9558936-7-4

First published 2012 by
Augur Press
Delf House,
52, Penicuik Road,
Roslin,
Midlothian EH25 9LH
United Kingdom

Printed by Lightning Source

Now Is Where We Are

Acknowledgements

I am deeply grateful for the continued love and support from my family and friends – both in respect of my illness, and of my creative endeavours.

My special thanks to John, Sue, Danny, Joe, Sandy, Helena, Hannah, Bridget, Sally-Ann and Tim; to Terence McGinnie; to Sue Bayliss; and to Gregory Parsons for the cover artwork.

Finally, I want to thank Augur Press for this publishing opportunity.

Cover image:
Ginkgo biloba is the world's oldest tree, and a 'living fossil'. It is revered worldwide for its rarity of form and ancient lineage, and has become a symbol of timeless beauty and endurance.

Author's note:

The poems in this collection grew from my depressive illness and subsequent experiences at the Priory Hospital. Readers should be reassured that the content of this collection is without reference to any particular person.

Contents

Foreword

Introduction

Foreword

by Dr Iain McGilchrist

Once read, these poems will always be your companions. By turns they move and delight with their beauty, wit and depth of fellow-feeling. That they should have come out of the heart of depression is an amazing and redemptive achievement. I am searching to remember anything quite like them – they have a tautness, a spare elegance, that at times reminds one of Emily Dickinson; at other times they have the gentle humour that only someone very sane can muster. And in all of them there is that combination of concern, sympathy and detachment which enables art, as it enables healing, to happen. These are the real thing.

Dr Iain McGilchrist is a psychiatrist, author, and former Oxford Literary Fellow. He currently holds a Staff Consultant post at The Priory Hospital, Hayes Grove, where he was Medical Director until 2004. His seminal work on brain hemisphere functioning, entitled *The Master and his Emissary*, was published by Yale University Press in 2009. His interests include the relationship between creativity and mental illness. I would like to thank Dr McGilchrist most sincerely for this kind endorsement, and for his medical expertise, which has been integral to my recovery. More about Dr McGilchrist can be seen at www.iainmcgilchrist.com

HL

Introduction

That there is a link between psychiatric illness and creativity seems widely accepted, although not completely understood. The 'black dog' of clinical depression has kept me intermittent company since my early teens, and I have often written prolifically while recovering from periods of depressive illness. So after the most recent and most acute episode, when I spent some time in the Priory Hospital, those closest to me weren't surprised by my sudden and rather frenetic poetic output.

This time, however, the impetus for writing poems was different. I had listened to, and later talked to, people of all ages, who were suffering from a wide range of physical and emotional difficulties. They provided the inspiration to express some of our shared truths – feelings and experiences in common with, and understood through, others.

*****

One young girl from the Eating Disorder Unit said: 'At moments I can see why and how to change – it's like a light going on – yet when I reach out for it, it eludes me.' [*The Awakening*]

A desperately depressed lady struggled to express how: 'Things that should be normal and nice – like light and sound and colour – are an ordeal.' [*The Colour Pink*]

A therapist explained: 'Depression is the opposite of expression. If we press things down inside, through fear or anger, inevitably we will reach a breaking point.' [*Words*; *Nothing Undoing; What If I Said*]

I learned that we can literally 'love too much' for our own good [*The Last Oasis*; *The Rescuer*]; that we need to establish clear boundaries in our relationships – with ourselves and with others [*Boundaries*]; and that we alone are responsible for 'owning' our emotions and choosing our behaviours [*Owning It*; *A Matter of Emphasis*]. This has provided a platform from which I can consider what love actually is; judge how much I can give of myself to others; and become more alert to my emotional states and their origins.

I found communion and understanding with unexpected people, in strange places – for example, with the anorexic girls in the Priory's smokers' hut [*Smoking at the Pariahs' Gazebo*]. Perhaps most importantly, I began to see that in the most terrible negatives there is strength and even humour to be found – if only we remain open to it [*Open Roads*; *The Fear of Letting Go; Briefly Bipolar*].

*****

I continue to become more truly who I am, and feel better. Although I am still writing, I have resisted the urge to go back and 'tweak' things in these poems that might be improved upon with hindsight. I feel that *Now Is Where We Are* should tell the truth of where I was *then*, while suggesting where I hope I'm going *now*.

If any of the poems in these pages speak to you, perhaps there's comfort in knowing that you're not alone.

My psychiatrist, Dr Iain McGilchrist, told me: 'Depression is an illness, as real as heart disease, and yet people remain ashamed to have it. They should know they are in good company. And however destructive and terrible it may be, it can also prove, in the long run, with the right support and treatment, to have provided a source of self-knowledge and spiritual connection, close to the heart of creativity.'

An Individual Diagnosis

His is a shadow dog
Mine a spiteful monkey
With discoloured curling claws
And eyes like fog

His is stubborn and morose
Mine clings onto my chest
And hawks its hiss and spittle
Flecks upon my breast

His is terminally sad
While mine is at once
Clamorous and bad

Are there no others to be had?

The monkey and the dog agree
That his is stuck with him
And mine is stuck with me

His is a shadow dog
Mine a spiteful monkey
With discoloured curling claws
And eyes like fog

The Awakening

I feel a friction spark
The reaches of my soul
A glinting at the dark
Horizon of its whole

I sense it with my heart
A pulse in embryo
The echo of a start
A bubble from below

It is so frail, so pure
So tenuously bright
It trembles like a tear
And shivers in the light

It will not flare for me
It will not catch and take
Yet it is there in me
Potentially awake

Its phosphorescent breath
A nascent clarity
New life within the death
Of possibility

Words

I am chock-full of words;
they crouch in flocks until I choose
to let their pinions beat,
when in an instant they are loosed

Like tiny Hitchcock birds
the frantic creatures dip and dart
and nip with needled beaks
the pulsing fabric of your heart

Your pain cannot be heard
through tangled wings that rake your face,
and every time you speak
they writhe inside your breathing space

I would have said that words
can never damage flesh and bone
if it were not for yours, that wreaked
such havoc on my own

Nothing Undoing

You cannot say the words then take them back.
A match ignited cannot help but burn,
nor, though the flame be snuffed, may it return
to its potential; red has changed to black.
You cannot launch a fleet with Helen's face
then judge another worth your Trojan war;
men need to know what they are fighting for.
Take faith away, and nothing takes its place
but ciphers more unfilled than faithlessness.
Some things once done cannot be done again;
hurt upon hurt conceives a different pain
which in its turn inflicts a new distress,
while others done cannot then be undone;
words may be said, but they are never gone.

Smoking at the Pariahs' Gazebo

We meet there every evening, silently
I do not smoke; this is a different me
Whose fingertips burn hot and red, and trace
An arc of embers to and from my face

She steps inside me and we start to breathe
We suck in every tendril, each frail wreath
We fill our lungs with nicotine and loss
And hold it in, and close our eyes, because

The others have arrived who don't exist
Young girls, their contours smudged into the mist
Transparent limbs and vulnerable wrists
And mouths that puff, but never have been kissed

Theirs is the acquiescence of despair
Exhaled as perfect smoke-rings in the air

Owning It

Kathryn won't refer to 'I' or 'me';
She speaks as 'one', occasionally 'we'.
She says, one ought not *this*,
One might feel *that*;
A sweet old civil service
Bureaucrat

Kathryn, it is time for you to own
The bitter carnage that is yours alone.
The agonising fissures
In the bone; the raw
Red howl of what is dead
And gone

Kathryn does not talk as 'one' or 'we';
She cries oh-god-it-hurts-it's-killing-me.
She says, I once had *that*,
And it was real;
Now *this* is who I am,
And how I feel

The Softest Touch

Surely nothing could be softer
than her muzzle
when she noses me to say

I'm here;
It's morning, are you
in *there?*

I cannot help but smile each time
the gentle wishbone
of her mouth finds mine

Because I know
this warm, this slightly
breath-damp

Loving, laden with velour
just spiced with bristle
and a hint of crumb, is not

The softest touch,
nor I the only one who's
in *there*

The Colour Pink

we know you like the colour pink; today
you tell us how you made it all the way
to M&S to buy that cardigan
it took more than an hour to try it on
the buttons are quite tiny and you still
get shaky from the meds, although that will
improve (the side-effects of ECT
can come and go, you've heard, 'quite randomly')
but what about the channels in your head
where matchless memories have leached and bled
together into one then into none
the loving living pinkness has it gone
and did it have a price tag like the one
still fastened to your brand new cardigan?

The Rescuer

They want me to protect myself
To be less nice for my own good
And nothing matters like my health
So I would do it if I could

The problem is the way I love
The all-not-nothing, sink-not-swim
The never ever good enough
To be like her and be with him

And how it hurts to feel the world
To know its darkness, take it in
To open like a leaf unfurled
And leave exposed my thinnest skin

In therapy they say I take
Much more than my heart should forgive
I worry that it will not break
And I must live, and I must live

i spy ...

you ask me what i see
each time i look at you
do i spy you and me

you ask me what we are
and where we're going to
and is it near or far

and are we truly real
and is it really true
and is this how i feel

well *is* it?

it's the same my love
i'm lonely too and
tired of playing this game

why can you never see
that when i look at you
my little i spies me

Games of Chance

You say there's something you must find;
The piece to fit your jigsaw heart.
I offered mine, you said its shape
Was nothing like the missing part.

Though I would change to make you whole
And mould myself to fill your space,
Still you indulge a piecemeal soul
And wear with pride the missing place.

Your puzzle never will be solved
By perfect, made-to-measure love;
You cheat yourself, you would do well
To know my best is good enough.

The Last Oasis

I cannot give you water, I have none.
You drank it all, my dear, your share and mine
As we lay bleached beneath a violent sun,
The last oasis desert-miles behind.
I cannot give you loyalty or trust,
You cannot give me back my peace of mind,
For what we were is only so much dust
Left here for the sirocco wind to find.
I cannot give you time. It has run out;
It would not stop within my careful hand;
And where I journeyed with my burnt-out heart
Was just a mirage, not the promised land.
I cannot give you love, for it has gone
The way of all the water. I have none.

What If I Said

I could have said to her
it is not love
that twists
his urgent fingers in your hair;
it is not love
that keeps him moving there

she could have said to me
I do not care

I could have said to her
it is not tenderness
he breathes
into your upturned face;
not wonderment;
he finds that in another place

she could have said to me
yet still he stays

I could have said
it is not right
it is not fair

instead I said
we should not fight;
it's good to share;

and what could she have said?

Open Roads

She gets no pleasure from the thought
Of driving fast tonight;
No longer likes the car he bought –
A gift to make things right
(Too little and too late); in short,
She has no appetite
For open roads.

She finds no freedom and no sport
In panicked, windblown flight
From places where her past is caught
Like cats' eyes by the light;
No future, when an end is sought
But always out of sight
On open roads.

But she is proud of how she fought
When it was worth the fight;
And she is blessed by what it brought
When it was at its height;
And so, she thinks, perhaps she ought
To drive again at night
On open roads.

Kristallnacht

It must end soon, this night of broken glass;
The wanton music of the axe will pass
And abaci of heartbeats count the cost,
Each bead an unimaginable loss.

Pluck out the shards and shivers from your eyes,
Witness the smithereens of what you prize
Reflected in the polished mastery
And blank indifference of cruelty.

Pray for the fortitude to stand as one
Beneath the sledgehammer, before the gun,
And when you fall together breathe the name
That keeps your legacy of love aflame.

For this is just one night, and it will pass;
To you, the victory of broken glass.

Note: Kristallnacht, also referred to as 'The Night of Broken Glass', was a series of attacks against Jews throughout Nazi Germany and parts of Austria on 9-10 November 1938. SA Storm troopers and civilians destroyed synagogues and Jewish homes and shops, leaving the streets covered with broken glass. Ninety-one Jews were killed, and 30,000 Jewish men taken to concentration camps.

A Matter of Emphasis

After all, history
Is a matter of emphasis,
I said. He said, I don't agree;
Things either happen or they don't.

But doesn't it depend,
I said, on how far back you go?
On context? No. There is an end
And a beginning, things are as they are

And you and me, he said,
We started *here*; for me it is
Quite clear: the day we went to bed
Was the first day of the affair.

But what about the last,
I said; was it the day you left
Without a backward glance, or afterwards,
When you begged for a final

Final chance? Because
As far as I can see, I said,
We are still making history.

He said, it isn't over.
I said, I don't agree.

The Fear of Letting Go

I am afraid
of letting go
the upturned palm
the tautened bow

the quick release
the breasted edge
the stall
the fall
the crackling ledge

I am afraid
of being hurt
the pinch of pain
the horsehair shirt

the end in sight
the faithless start
the slight
the flight
the paper heart

I am afraid
but do not run
the slantwise cheek
the coral sun

the wind may rouse
their fantail leaves
but stalwart
are the
ginkgo trees

Boundaries

There should be a book
On boundaries
On how we cross them
With a look

Beyond the border
Of the heart
On how they rarely finish
Where they start

On how we shrink them
With our fear
But as too far
Becomes too near

We love and give
Without restraint
No life to live
No time to take

Yes, there could be a bible
On the things
All checks and balances
And reckonings

Where stepping out
Is coming home
And running free
Is not alone

Where not enough
Can fill a space
And much too much
Has no such place

We do not need
To raise the bar
To measure up
To who we are

For in the book
There is a choice
To make the leap
Before the look

To swim the moat
And climb the wall
And breach the keep
While others fall

To find a way out
Of the maze
Back to the circle
Of our days

These are the boundaries
Of the heart
They do not finish
Where they start

The Letter I Mean to Write

I will write from me to me
to tell us both that, honestly,
while being miles away from perfect,
we are loved, and we are worth it.

I will have my Adult (A.)
inform my Vulnerable Child (V.C.)
that she and I are both okay,
and each of us needs both of me.

And when my Persecutor (P.)
intrudes to sneer, 'What, seriously?
you are a world away from perfect;
as for love, you're *so* not worth it,'

A. and V.C. then can write,
explaining to the P. within
that she is wrong, and we are right,
and we will let the best me win.

Two Tattoos

To the warrior,
the will to go the distance;
heart and acceptance.

Briefly Bipolar

He sat down next to me
And said
My name is
Ron

They think I'm manic
But I'm sure
They're
Wrong

I looked up but
He was
Already
Gone

Coming Back

Most of us who went away
are coming back. Some may stay,
while some will not return at all
they are so disparate and small

these are the fractions lost in space,
decimals without a place

Some are divided into two,
fifty per cent of me-plus-you
less the remainder of each heart
bisected, riven, cleft apart

the whole was infinitely more
than twice the half they were before

Others are gunning four-by-fours
or waging interstellar wars;
catching spindrift on the ark
in pairs, or waltzing in the dark

the spirit equal to the task,
no matter what the questions ask

And some are gentling those who fear
the negative which draws too near;
for living is the only test
when love will answer all the rest

most of us who went away
are coming back; and some may stay

The Gift

Held in the wet satin of yet-to-come
I was given a gift; an ordinary
handing-over, casual as a birthday
card from colleagues.

It was a heart, its charm
an unapologetic round redness
and the certainty of being mine.

Cheerful like a chocolate my gift shone;
with a candy shell it seemed impervious –
a talisman, a victory, a fist
of life to deflect all suffering;

I didn't taste the bittersweet blessing
till it swelled a second time, only to burst
and grow once more,

The gift in the giving, over and over
the heart which keeps loving.

For other titles from Augur Press
please visit

www.augurpress.com

Poems of Wartime Years by W N Taylor

ISBN 978-0-9549551-6-8   £4.99

My experience of World War 2 was in the Far East, but these are not 'war poems' in the ordinary sense. They are thoughts and memories of the periphery rather than the centre of action, and reflections afterwards in subsequent years, some pertaining to other wars, bearing the stamp of futility, cynicism, sadness and a flicker of hope. Before demobilisation I served for a short time in a prisoner-of-war camp in Scotland, attending to German prisoners. It was disconcerting to be back in civilian life. Peace was full of unease, and hardly seemed peaceful. The effect of the war on social life, and upon my reaction to it, was disturbing. Our culture had changed, and I felt not for the better. I was uneasy; and thinking moreover of the international unrest and subsequent wars, I wondered what it was all leading to. I still wonder.

Order from your local bookshop, amazon.co.uk or the augurpress website at www.augurpress.com

The Voice Within by Catherine Turvey

ISBN 978-0-9558936-3-6   £5.99

Creative writing is a wonderful way to express and deal with all sorts of emotions and feelings related to the real world we live in, and everyday life. I was inspired to put all my work together in a book, when family and friends requested copies of my work to keep or to show others. I felt that if my few words could help people in any way by bringing comfort, hope, or encouragement, then why not bring it together for all those who would be interested?

Catherine Turvey is thirteen years old.

Order from your local bookshop, amazon.co.uk or the augurpress website at www.augurpress.com